Marilyn *Monroe*

A POSTCARD BOOK ™

Running Press
Philadelphia, Pennsylvania

Postcard Book is a trademark of Running Press Book Publishers.

Canadian representatives: General Publishing Co., Ltd., 30 Lesmill Road, Don Mills, Ontario M3B 2T6. International representatives: Worldwide Media Services, Inc., 115 East Twenty-third Street, New York, New York 10010.

9   8   7   6   5   4   3   2   1
The digit on the right indicates the number of this printing.

ISBN 0−89471−766−9
Cover design by Toby Schmidt.
Interior design by Skagg.
Front and back cover photograph: Photofest.
Interior detail photographs: Photofest.

Typography by Commcor Communications Corporation, Philadelphia, Pennsylvania.
Printed and bound in the United States of America by Innovation Printing.

Every effort has been made to give credit to individual photographers when this information could be found.

This book may be ordered by mail from the publisher. Please add $2.50 for postage and handling. *But try your bookstore first!* Running Press Book Publishers, 125 South Twenty-second Street, Philadelphia, Pennsylvania 19103.

*S*he is the ultimate American love goddess, a paradox of moist-mouthed sexuality and the girl next door. She filled a need we didn't know we had, then left us craving more. The magical transformation of Norma Jean Baker into Marilyn Monroe reads like a fairy tale. Born in 1926 in Los Angeles, Norma Jean grew up during the Depression, shuttling between foster homes—sometimes abused, often neglected. At 16, she married her neighbor, James Dougherty. Shortly afterward, Dougherty enlisted in the merchant marines, and Norma Jean began working in an aircraft factory, where she was discovered by an Army photographer.

When World War II had ended, Norma Jean divorced Dougherty and began a modeling career which led to a film contract with Twentieth-Century Fox. Norma Jean Baker became the hopeful starlet Marilyn Monroe. She played bit parts in B movies, and when her scenes weren't lost in the cutting room, she usually received good reviews.

Many details of Marilyn's ascending career—the hit films, the charity benefits, the popping flashbulbs, the storybook weddings turned sour—are true of hundreds of other celebrities. Why is Marilyn the perennial star? Marilyn Monroe was the personification of glamour, an erotic vision of the good life after the war. She had zest, sophistication, and wit; her acting was respected; and even at her most sultry, there was a sweetness about her.

While Marilyn showed us the beauty of fantasy, she also taught us that fantasy isn't always enough: despite the diamonds and decolletage, she was just Norma Jean. Her death in 1962 revealed her private pain and foreshadowed the disillusionment of the coming decade.

Today, after so many years, America is still in love with Marilyn. She remains our brightest star, missed even by those too young to remember her.

Marilyn loved to cultivate her voluptuous, sultry image, but she didn't want to be limited by it.
Photograph: Photofest.

A POSTCARD BOOK ™
© 1989 by Running Press Book Publishers

Norma Jean Baker was born in Los Angeles on June 1, 1926. The identity of her father is unknown; her mother, a film cutter, was institutionalized in a mental hospital. From these bleak beginnings arose the immortal Marilyn Monroe. Photograph: Photofest.

Marilyn
Monroe

A POSTCARD BOOK™
© 1989 by Running Press Book Publishers

Norma Jean Baker's childhood was no field of clover. An illegitimate child, she spent most of her youth in loveless foster homes. Photograph: The Bettmann Archive.

Marilyn Monroe

A POSTCARD BOOK ™
© 1989 by Running Press Book Publishers

*T*he beauty before the beauty spot: young starlet
Marilyn Monroe. Photograph: Photofest.

Marilyn Monroe

A POSTCARD BOOK ™

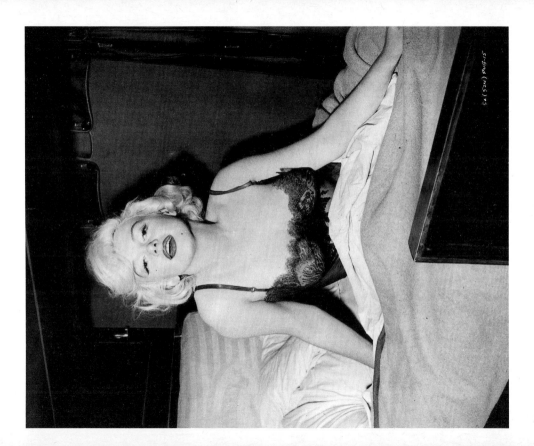

At home, Marilyn revealed that she wore only
Chanel No. 5 to bed, but as Sugar Kane in *Some Like
It Hot,* she donned something slightly more conservative.
Photograph: The Bettmann Archive.

A POSTCARD BOOK ™
© 1989 by Running Press Book Publishers

In the early '50s, Marilyn Monroe's career consisted of bit parts and pinups. By 1953, she was on top of the world – a star on the rise. Photograph: The Bettmann Archive.

A POSTCARD BOOK™

Marilyn "had a great talent for directing the entire impact of her personality at the lens," recalled photographer Philippe Halsman. Photograph: Photofest.

Marilyn Monroe

A POSTCARD BOOK™
© 1989 by Running Press Book Publishers

*I*n private, Marilyn Monroe was very shy, yet she always had a warm smile for the camera.
Photograph: Photofest.

A POSTCARD BOOK™
© 1989 by Running Press Book Publishers

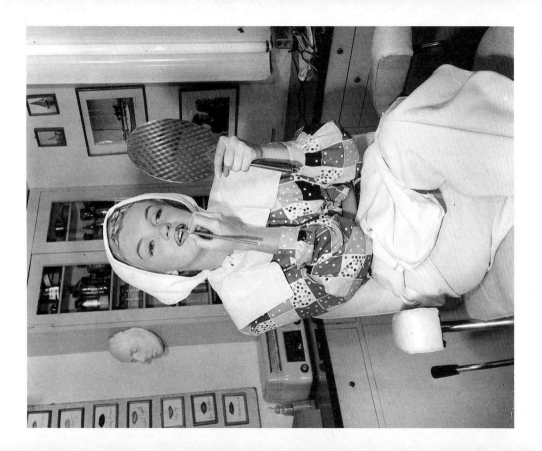

This publicity shot, taken in the makeup department of Columbia Pictures in 1947 or 1948, reveals that beauty came naturally to Marilyn. Photograph: The Bettmann Archive.

Marilyn Monroe

A POSTCARD BOOK ™

Shivering or shimmying, Marilyn captured the eyes of the world. She loved the attention, but regretted the lack of privacy that followed. Photograph: Photofest.

Marilyn
Monroe

A POSTCARD BOOK ™

Marilyn didn't need jewels to make her sparkle.
Her warmth appealed equally to men and women.
Photograph: The Bettmann Archive.

A POSTCARD BOOK ™
© 1989 by Running Press Book Publishers

A radiant Marilyn as she appeared in 1950, during the
filming of *All About Eve*. Her role was small, but the
film was critically acclaimed and widely seen.
Photograph: Photofest.

Marilyn
Monroe
A POSTCARD BOOK ™
© *1989 by Running Press Book Publishers*

Marilyn's biggest fan certainly wasn't the one concealed beneath the subway grate. The filming of this scene for *The Seven Year Itch* attracted more than 2,000 onlookers. Photograph: Photofest.

Marilyn Monroe

A POSTCARD BOOK ™
© *1989 by Running Press Book Publishers*

*S*ome of her costars and a few directors complained that she was difficult to work with, but to her fans, Marilyn was always pleasant. Photograph: The Bettmann Archive.

A POSTCARD BOOK™
© *1989 by Running Press Book Publishers*

The very picture of glamour, Marilyn Monroe had what Truman Capote called "this presence, this luminosity, this flickering intelligence." Photograph: Photofest.

A POSTCARD BOOK ™
© 1989 by Running Press Book Publishers

*F*ilm work wasn't steady early in Marilyn's career.
In the long gaps between films, Marilyn posed for pinups.
A nude calendar photo, for which she was paid $50,
created a stir when it was made public. Photograph:
The Bettmann Archive.

A POSTCARD BOOK ™
© 1989 by Running Press Book Publishers

Their storybook romance culminated in the wedding
of the decade when Marilyn Monroe and Joe Dimaggio,
The Yankee Clipper, were married on January 14, 1954.
Although the marriage didn't last through October, the
couple remained close friends. Photograph: Photofest.

Marilyn
Monroe

A POSTCARD BOOK ™
© 1989 by Running Press Book Publishers

*B*eauty and the beach? A high-spirited Marilyn Monroe frolics by the sea. Photograph: The Bettmann Archive.

A POSTCARD BOOK ™
© 1989 by Running Press Book Publishers

Marilyn Monroe appeared in 29 films during her 13-year career. In her first film, *Scudda-Hoo! Scudda-Hay!* (1948), Marilyn can be glimpsed rowing a boat in the background. She later played a wide range of characters, including a mentally disturbed baby-sitter and a showgirl. Photograph: Photofest.

A POSTCARD BOOK ™
© 1989 by Running Press Book Publishers

*A*lways aware of the camera, Marilyn was never "caught" at a bad angle. Equally relaxed in jewels or jeans, she created the image that she wanted the camera to see. Photograph: The Bettmann Archive.

A POSTCARD BOOK ™
© *1989 by Running Press Book Publishers*

On a bitterly cold day in Korea in February, 1954,
Marilyn warmed the troops (and later caught
pneumonia). Photograph: Dave Cicero/UPI
Bettmann Newsphotos.

Marilyn
Monroe

A POSTCARD BOOK ™
© 1989 by Running Press Book Publishers

*D*escribed by Norman Mailer as "the sweet angel of sex,"
Marilyn could seduce a nation with her eyes closed.
Photograph: Photofest.

A POSTCARD BOOK ™

On her way to becoming a major league talent in her own right, Marilyn posed for publicity photos in a number of unlikely situations. Photograph: Photofest.

Marilyn Monroe

As Grand Marshal of the 1952 Miss America Parade,
Marilyn thrilled the crowd in Atlantic City. Photograph:
UPI/Bettmann Newsphotos.

Marilyn
Monroe
A POSTCARD BOOK ™
© *1989 by Running Press Book Publishers*

When Marilyn was once asked why she didn't get a suntan, she replied, "I like to feel blonde all over." Photograph: Photofest.

A POSTCARD BOOK ™
© 1989 by Running Press Book Publishers

Not looking a day over 30, Marilyn Monroe arrives in
New York, June 2, 1956, one day after her 30th birthday.
Photograph: The Bettmann Archive.

A POSTCARD BOOK ™
© 1989 by Running Press Book Publishers

Mrs. Arthur Miller showed us that intellectual can be sexy. Throughout her career, Marilyn struggled against the notion that being blonde means being dumb. Photograph: Photofest.

Marilyn Monroe

A POSTCARD BOOK ™
© 1989 by Running Press Book Publishers

As the nearsighted husband-hunter in *How to Marry a Millionaire*, Marilyn surprised her critics by demonstrating a keen sense of comic timing. Photograph: Photofest.

A POSTCARD BOOK ™
© 1989 by Running Press Book Publishers

She started out as one of many hopeful starlets at Twentieth-Century Fox, but early photographs of Marilyn Monroe reveal the beauty and presence that would launch her as a superstar. Photograph: The Bettmann Archive.

Marilyn Monroe

A POSTCARD BOOK ™
© 1989 by Running Press Book Publishers

*I*n his eulogy to Marilyn, Lee Strasberg said, "In her own lifetime, she created a myth of what a poor girl from a deprived background could attain. For the entire world, she has become a symbol of the eternal feminine." Photograph: Photofest.

Marilyn Monroe

A POSTCARD BOOK ™